ST

CRUSADER FOR CHRIST

The Story of Billy Graham

by

JEAN WILSON

LUTTERWORTH PRESS
GUILDFORD AND LONDON

First paperback edition 1980

ISBN 0 7188 2490 3

PRINTED PHOTOLITHO IN GREAT BRITAIN
BY EBENEZER BAYLIS AND SON, LTD.
THE TRINITY PRESS, WORCESTER, AND LONDON

CONTENTS

1

DOWN ON THE FARM

BOOM! The sound of the guns could be heard right across the fields. Boom! Another shell screamed overhead. All around could be seen signs of war, for this was France in 1918. The Great War was drawing to a close but the noise of the battle could still be heard.

On a farm, the other side of the world in North Carolina, U.S.A., Billy Graham was born. His real name is William Franklin Graham but he soon became Billy Frank to his family. It would be many years before he was to visit France but one day he would go to that country as an evangelist to bring to them a message of peace, not just telling them of the peace that comes when wars cease but telling them of the peace which comes from God.

Billy was the eldest of two boys and two girls, and most of his childhood was spent on the farm helping his father with the cattle. It was not unusual for him to get up at three o'clock in the morning and run outside to help with the cows. Then, when everything was ready, he would go around the countryside delivering the milk. Then back to the farm to milk the cows all over again! He soon earned for himself the reputation of being the fastest milker in the county. He was kept so busy that he never had an opportunity to become lazy. Helping to plant the corn, clean out the shippons and all the jobs there are to do on the farm kept him out of mischief. But on a farm it is not all work and life can be fun as well. There were always rabbits to be chased and fish to catch and all the activities which most small boys love.

His mother had a great influence on him in his early life, and it was she who always wanted him to be a preacher. She encouraged him to read good books and appreciate music.

Billy grew up in a home where God was always put first. Every Sunday morning he would get up and go to Sunday School. It is usual in the United States for Sunday Schools to take place in the morning about 9.30 and, after Sunday School was over, Billy would go along to the morning service in the church. Sometimes the pews in the church became very hard and like most small boys Billy began to fidget and could not sit still. His father expected him to sit as quiet as a mouse, and his restlessness did not please the adults. One day he had hardly got outside after the morning service when his father took off his belt and gave him a good whipping. He sat still each Sunday after that.

When he was about four years old a great event happened which he was to remember a long time afterwards. A very famous preacher came to visit the town of Charlotte. This town was the nearest large community to the farm on which Billy lived, and he was taken along by his father to the meetings. Of course, he was much too young to realize that the man whom they were going to hear had preached to some of the largest crowds that had ever been known. All he knew was that this man was a tremendous baseball player. This was Billy's favourite game and it was his greatest ambition in life at that time to become a baseball player himself. It was not surprising that he went along willingly. He had heard many tales about the preacher, whose name was Billy Sunday. The preacher always started his services by running across the platform as hard as he could and sliding to the pulpit on his stomach, which was the way a baseball player would make a "home run". Billy Graham thought this would be tremendous fun and could hardly wait to see what happened. Billy's father threatened him that if he made one move he would see that Billy Sunday personally would administer the punishment. However, no threats were necessary on this occasion as young Billy was held spellbound throughout the entire service.

Schooldays came around all too soon. It was time for Billy to start his lessons. He didn't go to school very willingly on the first day and by the end of the day he was almost ready to leave school altogether. His mother had packed him some sandwiches for his lunch and he was told to eat them in the lunch break. Ten o'clock struck and all the class broke up for ten minutes.

"This must be lunch time," thought Billy, and eagerly ate all his sandwiches.

His mother had forgotten to tell him there would be a break in the middle of the morning and so, when the real lunch time came around he had nothing left to eat and had to go hungry until it was time to go home at the end of the afternoon. He took very great care to see that this did not happen any other day, but it was a very hungry Billy who rushed into the farm-house that evening ready for his tea. A few days later something else happened at school which made him feel he had had enough of school to last him for ever. An older boy did something to upset Billy. Billy, standing up for himself, made the mistake of shaking his fist at the older boy. Next day, Billy was cornered and given a good beating. The next day, and the next day after that, Billy had to suffer the same fate.

Eventually he found out he could run faster than the older boy, so every time the bully appeared on the scene Billy would start running. Although many fights still came along, Billy eventually settled down to become more peace loving.

When he was sixteen years old one of the greatest events in his life took place. Another preacher came to his town to conduct a series of meetings similar to the ones he had attended so many years before. This time the man's name was Mordecai Ham and he was holding an evangelistic campaign in Billy's home town. He was a very fiery man and hit the headlines in the local papers. Billy read them all out of curiosity and all his friends at school were talking about this preacher with the strange name.

"Will you come along to the meeting with me to-night?" one of his friends asked him one evening.

"Yes, I think I would like to see what goes on," replied Billy.

And so it was that, on that evening, Billy joined the 2,000 people who were already crowded into the specially built meeting place. When Billy got home that night he could not remember exactly what Mordecai Ham had said. All he knew was that he had sat listening with great attention as the evangelist told the crowd of their sins and of how they needed the Lord Jesus Christ to be their own Saviour. As he wended his way home he did a lot of thinking and all through the next day his thoughts kept going back to what he had heard in the meeting place the night before. Nothing could have kept him away from the meeting that evening, and night after night he returned to listen to the preacher. When Mordecai Ham had finished preaching he asked those who wanted to accept the Lord Jesus Christ as their own Saviour to come forward to the front of the pulpit. As Billy heard this each evening something inside him was strangely disturbed. He could not explain what was happening to him. All he knew was that all the preacher said seemed to be directed at him.

One night, in order to escape the words of the evangelist, Billy went to sit in the choir. He found himself seated next to a young man named Grady Wilson, who introduced him to his brother. The two Wilson brothers and Billy became firm friends and have remained friends all through their lives. The move into the choir did not work out quite as Billy had planned. As Mordecai Ham again asked those to come forward who wanted to start a new life Billy could stand it no longer, and simply and quietly went forward to learn more of what it meant really to be a Christian. That night, two or three hundred people were already there, and a deep sense of peace and joy flooded over him. He went home that evening with a new spring in his step, knowing in his heart that this was just a beginning. He still had a lot to learn and, in the years that followed, his parents tried to help him. His mother invited visiting evangelists to stay in their home. He learned a great deal from them.

The first time he stood up in public and spoke about what it was like to be a Christian was in a very unusual place. One of the evangelists who stopped with the Grahams was visiting a jail in North Carolina and took young Billy along with him. As he was talking to the prisoners, he turned and introduced Billy and said, "Here's a young man who can tell you what it's like to be converted." Although he had never made a speech before, Billy stood with trembling knees and told those men in jail of his experience.

Billy had his first attempt at earning his living just after leaving High School when he was eighteen years old. He longed to earn some money of his own, and when a friend of his told him he had just become Sales Manager for a brush company, the idea of helping to sell brushes sounded great fun to an eager young man. So Billy started going from door to door trying to convince everyone that they ought to have one of these brushes. He became so convinced that his brushes were the best that he told all the housewives who opened the door that no home could possibly afford to be without one. He had one hair-raising experience one day when an irate housewife threw a jug of water at him from an upstairs window. Fortunately, he saw the water coming and managed to dodge to one side and was only splashed with a few drops. This made him realize that selling was not all the fun he thought it was going to be.

He had now decided he did not want to follow his father and go into farming but felt he should continue his education by going to college. Eventually he arrived at the Florida Bible Institute. Florida is in the southern part of the United States with a wonderful climate, very warm in the winter and very hot indeed in the summer. The Bible School occupied one half of a large hotel, so the students were expected to work in the hotel in their time off to help pay for their education. They polished shoes and worked in the grounds and helped in the kitchen. He was so good at washing up that he became known as the fastest dishwasher in the college. Billy had not been at the college very long before he had his first lesson in what it really means to pray. The founder of the college called all the students together and told them the college desperately needed more money.

"We are turning to God for help," he said, "and I want all of you to join me in prayer."

All day long the students prayed, believing that God would supply their need. A telegram arrived at the college that evening from a man who said he felt somehow that he ought to send a cheque for $10,000 for the college. How this experience helped Billy at the beginning of his Christian life.

During that summer Billy was asked to help at a conference centre near the college. One day a visiting minister asked him if he would preach at a nearby Baptist Church.

"I do not know how to preach," said Billy timidly.

The minister was not to be put off, as he said "We will pray and God will help you." Unknown to the minister, Billy had secretly prepared an outline of four sermons. He was too frightened to sleep that night and went over and over the sermons in his mind until he knew them by heart. The next evening this very frightened young man stood shaking before the congregation as he was about to preach his first sermon. Somehow or other things did not go quite as he had expected because almost before he had begun to speak he found he had gone right through his first sermon.

"Whatever shall I do?" he thought.

He did the only thing he could do, and that was to go into his second sermon. In no time at all he had come to the end of his second sermon, and in desperation went on to the third. All too soon all that he had prepared in the third sermon had gone, and he had to start on his fourth and last sermon. At the end of eight minutes he was very confused and had to sit down because he had run out of words. By the end of the evening he was convinced he was not meant to preach. For weeks he wrestled with this problem and the more he thought about it the more sure he became that God must have some other purpose for his life.

One evening he was out walking on the golf course that surrounded the college. These thoughts were still troubling him. But as he stepped out into the moonlight on the last green he felt in some remarkable way that God really did want him to preach.

Falling to his knees he prayed, "O God, if you want me to preach, I will do it."

It was one thing to be convinced that he was to preach, however, and quite another to find somewhere to preach. All preachers have to have an invitation before they can speak, and as week followed week still no invitations came in. Billy knew that the Head of a mission in one of the towns in

Florida used to come to the college each week to choose a student to preach to his mission. Billy would go out of his way to make himself known to this man and to talk to him but always someone else would be chosen. One day, however, Billy was asked to go along and speak to the children. All must have gone well for him on this occasion for he was asked back a second time and soon he was preaching each weekend.

Just as the Second World War was breaking Billy, nearly 21 years old, was ordained as a minister. He soon discovered that being a minister was not quite as wonderful as he had thought it would be. The ministry meant a mixture of responsibilities and failures. He could now baptize people, conduct marriages and bury people. He also found he could enjoy certain privileges in the United States. He could travel at half price on the railways. He could play golf free at many courses. He could get his clothes cleaned at 10% off. All these things are a great help to a young minister who is not paid very much. Billy decided he would continue his education, so the next term found him in the north of the United States, near the city of Chicago, studying at Wheaton College. It was whilst he was here that some very interesting and important things happened to him.

2

THE NEW BEGINNING

IN the United States, most students have to have a job so that they can earn money to pay their way through college. Whilst Billy was at Wheaton, he met a young man who was working his way through college by driving a truck and dashing around Chicago in his spare time delivering and picking up everything and anything. He badly needed an assistant, and Billy badly needed a job, and so he offered Billy 50 cents an hour. This seemed too good an opportunity to miss and Billy jumped at the job. In the afternoon when they had no classes they could be found both very dusty and dirty moving everything that came their way.

It was on one of the days they were loading up the truck that Billy's friend introduced him to a lovely young girl who was later to become Mrs. Billy Graham.

In December, 1941, the United States of America entered the Second World War. Billy wanted to become an army chaplain but he was informed he would have to finish his college education first and then take a church for one year and be its minister before he could qualify. He met a young publisher, who suggested Billy should become the minister of his home church in Western Springs, Illinois. Billy was thrilled to receive this invitation for it meant he would be able to take a further course at Chicago University and also get the one year's experience that he needed to qualify for the Army chaplaincy. That following summer he and Ruth were married and started their life together working in a little church in Western Springs. The salary was very small and they had a hard time to make ends meet. In order that he might gain more experience Billy would accept any preaching engagements that came his way.

One day he was preaching in a little church in Elyria, Ohio. He had just twenty-one dollars in his pocket, a twenty dollar bill and a one dollar bill. As usual, during the service, the collection was taken and the plate came round to where Billy was sitting. It is a little strange to ask the preacher for a collection but it happened on this occasion. Billy was a little taken aback and fumbled in his pocket for the one dollar bill. Imagine his amazement when he saw with horror that the note dropping on to the plate was the twenty dollar bill. A verse in the Bible says "God loveth a cheerful giver" but Billy was not exactly cheerful on this occasion. As he sat at the front of the church, he could almost hear the ushers talking amongst themselves at the back and wondering where this rich young preacher got all his money. He just closed his eyes and prayed and asked God to uphold the promise that He would restore it manifold. His prayers were soon answered, for at the end of the service the ushers handed him a railway ticket back to his home and a cheque for ninety-five dollars.

All over America churches broadcast their own radio programmes regularly every day of the week. One such broadcast which was very popular was called "Songs In The Night". This was broadcast every Sunday evening and lasted about three-quarters of an hour. Churches which put on such broadcasts have to pay the costs for the time they are on the air, and this particular programme cost about one hundred and fifty dollars each week. A man called Dr. Torrey Johnson was responsible for "Songs In The Night", which came from his church in Chicago every Sunday.

One day he telephoned Billy and asked if he would like to take over the programme, the financial side as well. Billy's church was not very prosperous but in faith they accepted the challenge and went on the air. God honoured their faithfulness, for the money to pay for the radio time came in as well.

This broadcast was also the means of bringing Billy into contact with a man who has been with him ever since as his singer, George Beverly Shea. When the programme first started, Billy realized he would need a good singer, and knowing that Mr. Shea was a gifted man Billy decided to call on him at his office. His secretary said he could not see anyone on that day, but Billy was not to be put off. He just opened the door of Mr. Shea's office and walked straight in. He did not mean to be rude but just felt in his own mind that this was the right thing for him to do. After much discussion, George Beverly Shea finally agreed to come along to the opening night and he has been singing with Billy Graham ever since.

A few weeks later, Torrey Johnson again contacted Billy Graham. He had just founded the Youth for Christ movement, which soon spread to all parts of the world. Torrey Johnson wanted Billy to preach at the enormous Orchestra Hall in Chicago. Billy was dumbfounded.

"Of all the preachers in the country, why pick on me to preach at this important service?" he thought.

However, he carefully prepared what he had to say, and when he reached the hall his knees were knocking beneath him and he found the largest audience he had ever seen. The Youth for Christ movement began to grow with great speed and Billy found he was receiving more and more invitations to preach in different parts of the country.

Billy was still hopeful, however, of becoming a chaplain to the American Forces, and just as his name had gone on a waiting list to attend a school for chaplains he became ill and for six weeks lay in bed—with mumps. This seemed a very childish complaint for a grown man to go down with, just at the time when this important event was opening up before him. But God had other plans for His servant and it was not in God's plan that Billy should become an army chaplain. Just as he was recovering from his illness a listener to his radio programme sent him a cheque so that he could take his wife and go on a holiday to recover completely in Florida. This was really God at work, for when he reached Florida he found Torrey Johnson was already there and the two men spent a long time discussing a plan about which Torrey Johnson felt very deeply. He wanted to organize youth rallies throughout America, and eventually the world, and he wanted Billy to become a full-time organizer and evangelist. This was something Billy had not thought about, and he and his wife spent a long time praying over the problem, and finally they found the way clear for them. So Billy accepted the offer and became the first Vice-President of Youth for Christ. It was about this time that Billy added another member to his team. He was invited to address a conference near Montreat, where his wife's parents lived. The music director didn't appear and the meeting was due to begin.

"Would you like to announce your own hymns?" asked the organizer.

"Perhaps there is someone visiting the conference who could do it," replied Billy.

He was introduced to a young man who looked every inch an athlete. Actually the young man was on his honeymoon and his name was Cliff Barrows.

Neither of the two men realized that night that this was the beginning of a partnership which would last until the present day.

Throughout the ages it has always seemed that a famous evangelist has always had an equally famous songleader. No one can mention the name of D. L. Moody without the name of Ira D. Sankey coming to mind. In the same way Cliff Barrows has become Billy's right-hand man and he leads the whole of the service each evening during a Crusade right up to the time when Billy steps to the microphone to begin his message.

Although their meeting seemed like an accident,

Billy believes that God sent Cliff Barrows and each one of the other men who make up his team.

It was as an evangelist for Youth for Christ that Billy Graham came to Britain for the first time. With a team of men he travelled throughout the country preaching in all sorts of places. By this time the Second World War had just ended but food rationing was still in operation in England. Billy always likes to tell the story of how one morning in Wales they were given a stewed tomato for their breakfast. This did not seem much for hungry men but Billy was always most grateful, for the people they stayed with gave of their best.

When he returned to the United States after his first trip abroad, he was summoned to the bedside of Dr. W. B. Riley, who was President of the North Western School in Minneapolis.

"You are the man who will be my successor," Dr. Riley told him, but Billy was ill at ease.

He told the sick man he could not make any such promise. After much persuasion, he finally agreed that if Dr. Riley should die he would replace him until a more suitable President could be found. A few weeks later the telephone rang with the sad news that Dr. Riley was dead and Billy found that he was now the new President of the North Western School. In the United States the President of a school is rather like a Headmaster, and North Western School was a Bible School with about eight hundred pupils. How could he possibly do all the jobs he was called upon to do well? He was still travelling around as an evangelist for Youth for Christ and now he was the head of a large Bible College as well. It was not surprising that he found he was spending more and more time away from the college as he was called upon to speak at meetings throughout the length and breadth of the United States.

He was to continue in this position for some time longer, as he strove to cut himself into two or three different parts to do all the jobs he was called upon to undertake.

3

ON THE AIR

THE fastest growing city in the United States has witnessed many great spectacles. Los Angeles is a unique city—in fact it is not one city but a collection of several different cities made up into what is known as Greater Los Angeles, bounded on one side by the Pacific Ocean and on the other by the San Bernardino mountains. A pall of smoke can often be seen hovering in the sky. This "smog" can make a person's throat burn and eyes smart, although one would sometimes hardly know that the smog existed. It is caused by the fumes from the motor cars, which cannot escape out to sea because the prevailing wind blows the fumes back again. Nor can they escape eastwards over the mountains because they are too high. So there is nothing left but to hang motionless over the city until the wind changes and they can be blown over the Pacific Ocean. The whole area of California has seen great developments in its short history from the time of the first settlers to the present day twentieth-century bustle. A new person every ninety seconds comes to live in California.

This then was the setting for the first really big Crusade that Billy Graham held. When he arrived in the city at the start of the meetings he found placards everywhere announcing the Crusade in "the largest tent in the world". Prayer partners had been enrolled all over the city and had been praying for these meetings well in advance. There seemed to be something in the air that no one could define. The Crusade was scheduled to run for three weeks and all went well for that time, although nothing spectacular occurred. And then something remarkable happened. Up to that time the newspapers had not paid much attention to what was taking place in their midst, but when Billy arrived at the tent for the fourth Friday of the meetings he found the place swarming with journalists and photographers. They shot questions at him and pictures of him in quick succcssion. The next day the Crusade was front page news in newspapers all across America and thousands of people swarmed to the meetings just to see what all the uproar was about. Perhaps they did come because of the publicity but many heard the story of how Jesus Christ had come to the earth and had died for their sins. They heard, too, of how they could become new people by believing this message and by asking Jesus to come into their lives. Many hundreds of people did just this in those days in Los Angeles.

Among the many well-known people who had a complete change of their lives after attending one of the meetings was a man called Jim Vaus. He was a notorious gangster and had been threatened that he would be killed. The rest of the criminals thought he would tell too many of the underworld secrets after he gave up his life of crime. Today, Jim Vaus runs a club for boys in one of the tough areas in New York's Harlem area. Had it not been for one of these meetings in Los Angeles perhaps he would still have been a wire tapper, one who could tap telephone wires to learn of important happenings and use the information for criminal ends.

And so Billy finished his meetings in Los Angeles and began to prepare to visit another part of America. This time Portland, Oregon, was his port of call and in that city a special meeting place was built for the series of meetings which Billy planned to hold there. Something happened in Portland that was to change the whole course of Billy's life. As the meetings progressed from day to day, two advertising men began to plague Billy, hoping he would become interested in a radio programme. They wanted Billy to go on the radio in a big way and so persistent were they that in the end Billy had to tell his friend, Grady Wilson, to get rid of the two men in some way. They had told Billy that the radio programme would cost 25,000 dollars (about £8,500) and then each week would cost another 7,000 dollars. The men were so persistent that Billy had to leave his hotel on one occasion by the fire escape to avoid meeting them. Eventually they realized that it was no use staying any longer and prepared to leave. As the two men were about to leave their hotel room and return home, Billy turned to them and said, "If I should get 25,000 dollars by midnight tonight I will take it as an answer to prayer and go on the radio."

The visitors were so sure that he was asking the impossible that they turned and left the hotel and went to the airport to catch a plane.

At the meeting that night Billy told the audience about the two men who had been to visit him and of their idea for the radio programme. When he mentioned that he would need 25,000 dollars he could hear some of the audience laughing. He did not actually make a plea for the money but just put the facts of the case before the audience and left it at that. After the service the people streamed to him with cheques, cash and promises. Billy was overwhelmed as they added up the money and found the final figure was just—23,500 dollars. He did not know what to think.

"Could God have given me the money, or is this a trick of the devil to tempt me to go against God's will?" These thoughts went round and round in his mind. He just did not know what to think.

It was nearly midnight when Billy and his friends got back to the hotel where they were staying. They were feeling rather let down because in great faith and believing that God would answer their prayers they had asked for 25,000 dollars. They could not quite understand why they had come so close to the figure they needed but not close enough. As they went through the foyer of the hotel one of the porters on duty called out to Mr. Graham that there were some letters for him. Billy stood looking down at the envelopes in his hand and saw that one of them was postmarked two days earlier from Texas. With fingers that trembled and fumbled with the envelope, he slit open the flap and found inside 1,000 dollars from someone he had never met in his life but who had heard him preach and felt that Billy ought to be heard on radio. The other two envelopes each contained a cheque for $250 from two people who had not been able to stop behind at the meeting but who had left their gifts at the hotel on their way home. This was indeed a miracle.

It was not yet midnight as Billy, fighting back his tears, turned round and saw the two men who had earlier gone to the airport striding through the door once again.

"We went to our plane," the two men said, "but something told us not to go on. So we have come back."

Billy put his hands on their shoulders.

"Sign up for those programmes," he said, "because we have the 25,000 dollars right here."

So the Hour of Decision was born, and today this radio programme can be heard on nearly one thousand stations throughout the world each week. It brings the message of Jesus Christ to many thousands of people in all different countries and from many walks of life. In some parts of the world, radio is the only means that many people have of hearing the Gospel preached. In other parts of the world people, even today, find it difficult to be able to attend church, and their own room becomes their church as they listen to the preacher's voice over the radio. Others are ill or old and find it difficult to leave their homes on a Sunday and to these people too their radio set becomes the preacher's pulpit. It is difficult for those who live in England to understand fully how these radio programmes work. In America, and in other countries of the world, it is possible to buy time on the radio in order to put out whatever kind of programme you would like.

So it is that even today Billy is able to buy this time on these many hundreds of radio stations in order to preach the Gospel. Of course, he does not buy it himself any longer because after he had signed up for these radio programmes he realized that he could not handle all the many details which would result from this by himself. He decided, therefore, to form an Association so that other men and women could handle all the day-to-day activities which would result from the programme and leave him free to preach his sermons. At that time he could not foresee that there would come a day when the office he established in Minneapolis would handle many thousands of letters a day from people all over the world who listened to Billy on the Hour of Decision radio programme. This office is able to help these people if they have problems, and many people write in each day asking for help and advice.

After the meetings in Portland, Billy carried on in all the other activities in which he was engaged. He was trying to do too many jobs at once. One day as he was walking in the mountains near his home a verse of a hymn came to his head.

> "Rescue the perishing, care for the dying,
> Snatch them in pity from sin and the grave.
> Weep o'er the erring ones, lift up the fallen,
> Tell them of Jesus the Mighty to save."

Suddenly he knew that God was telling him to spend his life in telling other people in every corner of the world of God's love for them. He knew he must concentrate on this and give himself to it wholeheartedly. With this thought in mind he immediately sat down and wrote his resignation to the Bible School. He was determined, with God's help, to fulfil this call. His dedication would take him to every part of the world, to preach in every continent. He knew it would mean separation from his wife and from his family for a long period of the year. He knew without any shadow of doubt that this was what God would have him do.

4

LONDON LISTENS

"MANOR HOUSE! Manor House!" The voice echoed along the platform of the underground station as a train shuddered to a halt. "Whish." The doors opened almost noiselessly and suddenly the platform was alive with crowds of people jostling good-humouredly for the exits.

Once outside the station they were met with a cold, wet night and a hint of snow in the air. Umbrellas raised, they hurried along, very much like any other crowds coming out of an underground station on their way to their nice cosy homes and a good meal after a hard day's work. But this crowd was rather different, for their destination was not a house, but Harringay Arena.

Usually Harringay Arena had been the scene of circuses and boxing matches, but today chairs had been put onto the floor of the arena, thus making the accommodation much larger than it usually was. The crowds had gathered to listen to a young American evangelist who had arrived in England to a storm of newspaper publicity. Some of the publicity was good, but some of it was rather nasty. It was March 1954.

Billy Graham had come to England and Harringay Arena at the invitation of a group of men and ministers of the churches who felt that England needed the message that Billy was able to give. This was the first time that he had accepted an invitation to speak outside America on such a large scale.

"Why don't you stay at home?" was a frequent question put to him by the newspaper reporters.

"Don't you think you're needed more in your own country?" And so the questions continued. But Billy was not dismayed for God had told him to go to London and he knew that He would help him through this difficult time. All across the Atlantic on the boat, Billy had had time to think of the tremendous challenge that was before him. But he was confident that people in England needed to know of God's love and of how He could change their lives, just as much as the people of America. Nevertheless, he knew that a time of great difficulty lay before him.

It was not until he had stepped off the boat that a word of good wishes came to him, and this was from a very unexpected source. A customs officer, usually very aloof and stiff, turned to Billy after looking through his suitcases and said to him, "Welcome to England, sir. We need you."

March 1st 1954! A day that will live long in Billy's memory. The night of the first meeting in Harringay and no one really knew what to expect.

"Would anyone turn out on such a wet night?" Billy thought as he sat in his hotel room preparing himself for the night ahead.

Mrs. Graham was with her husband during the day trying to help him, trying to make him understand that, no matter what lay ahead, God had a purpose in it all.

The meeting was due to begin at 7 p.m., and at 6 p.m. a phone call came through to the hotel, where Billy and his wife were waiting, from Harringay Arena.

"Nearly 200 newspaper reporters are here, and they're all gunning for you," said the voice at the other end of the phone.

Billy's heart began to fail.

"But surely," he thought, "God has not brought me all across the Atlantic for this."

Snow began to fall and Billy became even more depressed.

"Why should people bother to come out on a night like this?" he thought.

Then another call came through.

"The arena is only about one-fifth full and the photographers are taking pictures of the empty seats." His heart sank even lower.

Suddenly it was time to go, and as he and his wife prayed together a strange peace and calm came over them. Billy then realized with a great force that all around the world groups of people had been praying for just this occasion. Only that morning he had received two hundred cables from every part of the world telling him that in India, Singapore, Korea and many parts of the United States, people were praying for London. No matter what happened God was in control and knew all about the situation.

They climbed into their car and wended their way through the dark, cold streets of North London to the Arena. Then they saw a remarkable sight. People were streaming into the ground next door where greyhound racing was advertised to take place and not a single soul seemed to be going into the Arena. Before they could fully take in the scene, one of Billy's friends came running over to the car.

"The arena's jammed full," he said. "Every seat is taken."

It seemed that he could not believe himself what he had just said and had to repeat "The place is jammed. The building is full to overflowing and thousands are standing in the street on the other side of the building."

"Where did they come from so quickly?" Billy asked in surprise.

"I don't know," came the answer. "But here they are and just listen to them singing."

Through the walls of the building came the sound of thousands of voices raised in praise and thanksgiving.

Billy walked into the arena and up on to the platform in great humility. And when he got up to preach he took as his text probably the most well-known verse in the whole Bible, John 3: 16: "For God so loved the world. . . ." He told the thousands of people there that God loved them, and that no sin could escape the eye of God. He told them that the only way back to God is through Jesus Christ. At the close Billy asked for all those who wanted to be sure of the love of God for themselves and who wanted to start a new life to come forward, and as the choir sang, "Just as I am," 178 people responded and wended their way to the front of the huge arena.

This was only the beginning. Night after night that great arena was crowded with people who queued for hours to get seats. And some who could not get seats by the ordinary means managed to slip in through the back doors as parties of choir members arrived to take up their positions.

On one Saturday afternoon during the Crusade, a great crowd of children, snuggling down into their coats to keep warm, waited with almost baited breath to catch a glimpse of their favourite cowboy hero. Harringay Stadium had a great air of expectancy as the restless children waited for the great moment. Suddenly up one of the entrances a horse pranced into the picture and on his back none other than Roy Rogers, the famous cowboy star. His equally famous horse, Trigger, performed to the wild delight and enthusiasm of the audience.

But this was no ordinary cowboy scene, for Roy Rogers, his wife, Dale Evans, and other members of their party were there on a special errand. They had come to tell the children about the love of the Lord Jesus and before they left the stadium that cold afternoon 10,000 hands had been raised asking for prayer and 10,000 gospels of John had been issued to the children there.

For three months Billy preached to capacity crowds, and one final service was planned for Wembley Stadium. So great was the request for tickets that another stadium had to be booked across the other side of London at White City.

Then the committee of men who were responsible for arranging all the details of the meetings were faced with the problem of how to hold two final meetings on one day.

By the time the day came, both stadiums had "sold out" notices. It was a drab, chilly day and the rain came down in a steady drizzle as Billy drove to White City. A special platform had been erected at one end of the ground and it was from here that the service was conducted. 65,000 people sheltering under a multitude of umbrellas heard Billy preach that afternoon in White City.

Then, when the meeting was over, the police tried to clear a way for the bus which was to take the team to Wembley. Empire Stadium, Wembley, has a very special meaning for the vast majority of people who hear the name. It means the home of the FA Cup Final, and the stadium often sees sport there of one kind or another played on its famous turf. This turf is very special and is looked after and pampered by the groundsmen all through the year. Only a very few highly favoured people are allowed to go anywhere near this favoured piece of grass. But on the occasion of the last meeting that Billy was to address in England in 1954 something unheard of happened. Every seat in the great stadium was filled, and had been for hours before the scheduled start of the meeting. Then the officials unlocked the gates to allow thousands of people who had been waiting outside to swarm in and actually sit on the famous grass. When the doors were finally locked it was found that the stadium was accommodating 122,000 people. This was an unforgettable sight as high above the stadium the flags of America and Britain floated in the breeze. The huge score board had been covered over and emblazoned across it were the words, "Jesus said, I am the Way, the Truth and the Life."

After Billy had preached, the Archbishop of Canterbury offered the closing prayer, and then the great company present joined in a few verses of "Abide With Me". This was a great ending to twelve weeks of modern crusading. When the meeting was finally over, Billy walked away extremely tired. He had lost a great deal of weight during the three months he had been in England.

On the following Monday morning he was preparing to leave when the telephone rang.

"Sir Winston Churchill would like you to come to lunch tomorrow," the voice said.

"I'm sorry," Billy replied, "but it's impossible. I'm taking a train tonight."

When he had rung off he realized with horror

that because he was so tired he had just turned down an invitation from the Prime Minister.

Within a few minutes the phone rang again. "Could you come today at twelve?"

Billy dressed rapidly and shot over to No. 10 Downing Street. He was received by Sir Winston—they had lunch together and discussed world affairs.

* * *

"Can you see anything?" The woman on the station platform addressed her friend.

"I think someone's coming along," her friend replied as together they craned their necks. They had been waiting a long time and were very tired.

Such a vast crowd was gathered at St. Pancras Station that those on the edge could see very little of what was going on. Billy was leaving England bound for Europe to preach again to thousands of people in a fortnight's tour of European cities. As his train pulled out of the station the vast crowd on the platform sang with their hearts full of thanksgiving to God, "To God be the glory, Great things He hath done."

A great many people can tell of the amazing things that have happened to their lives since they went to Harringay. There was one girl—let's call her Kathleen—who experienced a completely new change in her life. Kathleen was a nurse in a hospital in London and she spent all her spare time looking for excitement. One day she saw a poster saying "Hear Billy Graham". At first she thought he was a dance-band leader, but she couldn't get that poster out of her mind. In the hospital she found a tract lying around and, though she laughed about it with her friends, she took it to her room to read.

Throughout the day that followed she seemed to see the poster in her mind and, near the beginning of the Crusade, she sneaked off alone to Harringay Arena. Kathleen arrived late and sat at the back, and while Billy was preaching she heard these words, "You have come here tonight dissatisfied—looking for a purpose in life. You could leave here a new person." This was just what she was wanting and at the end of the meeting she rushed back to the Nurses' Home. In the quietness of her own room she fell on her knees and gave her heart to the Lord.

From that day a new life began for Kathleen. God spoke to her about becoming a missionary and so she entered a training college. After a time of hard work and study she sailed for South America, where today she lives with just one other girl in a small forest town.

"This is my story," says Kathleen. "It could have been very different. I believe in miracles for I have seen many since that greatest one in my own life way back in Harringay Arena."

5

INTO ALL THE WORLD

THE next year saw Billy and his team back in Britain once again. Such a great impact had been made upon the British people that an invitation was given to Billy to conduct six weeks of meetings in Kelvin Hall, Glasgow.

The people of Scotland soon took Billy to their hearts. As night followed night Kelvin Hall was full of Scotsmen with ears and hearts open to receive the message.

Across the front of the building the biggest poster ever erected in Great Britain blazed its message to the City of Glasgow. Measuring 100 feet by 25 feet and in letters 3 feet high the motto of Glasgow lent an added impact to the atmosphere. "Let Glasgow flourish by the preaching of the Word and the praising of His Name," it proclaimed.

On Good Friday Billy was rather nervous. He had good reason to be, too, for he had been asked to let the Crusade service from Kelvin Hall be televised and broadcast simultaneously. It was the very first time that, anywhere, a live telecast of a Crusade service had been attempted in the world.

The broadcast was a tremendous success. It was seen by ten million viewers, and there were some remarkable cases of people accepting Christ into their lives by their own firesides.

In one public tavern over thirty customers watched the service on television and not one single drink was bought in that hour.

At the end of that time the team travelled south for a week of meetings in the vast Wembley Stadium. During the time Billy was in Glasgow he received a great surprise. One day a note was handed to him and when he opened it he could hardly believe his eyes. It was an invitation from the Queen. Queen Elizabeth was requesting that Billy should preach at Windsor Castle and afterwards he was asked to have lunch with Her Majesty and Prince Philip. This was a great honour and Billy spent a long time preparing the sermon he was going to preach on the Sunday in Windsor. It was all set out in large type so that he would be able to refer to his notes whilst preaching, but when he was ushered into the chapel at Windsor he found to his great horror that there was no pulpit!

"Whatever can I do?" he thought.

In the end he did the only thing possible. He stuffed the notes into his pocket and preached from memory.

Just prior to his visit with the Queen, Billy preached for one week in Wembley Stadium. The rain came down most of the time, but still many hundreds of people came to give their lives to the Lord Jesus Christ.

So it was time for Billy to leave England again. He embarked upon what many people described as a far too exhausting tour. For four weeks he toured Europe and preached in twelve cities in seven different countries. In all this time, of course, he had to preach through an interpreter—someone who stood alongside him and, after every few words that Billy spoke, translated those words into the language of the country. Sometimes this can be very difficult, because when the speaker comes to the end of a sentence he has to wait until that sentence is translated before he can go on speaking. Many people find it difficult to think in this way because what they want to say is broken up into pieces. Billy has to do exactly this when he preaches in any foreign country. First of all he has to say a few words in English, and then wait until the interpreter has translated those words. Then he can go on to the next words, and so on. In some parts of the world—in Africa, for instance, where there are several local dialects—it is not unusual for there to be two or even three interpreters. This means, that whatever Billy says has to be put in very simple language so that the sequence of thought is not lost.

So it was that in Billy's tour of Europe he had to have an interpreter in every town where he preached. As well as being difficult, he found that it sometimes led to very funny events. Often there is not an exact word in another language corresponding with our English word, especially if we use what is called idiomatic speech. This can often produce some head-scratching on the part of the interpreter, who has to be very quick with his translations. When Billy was in one country recently he had a very funny experience. He was telling the audience the story of John the Baptist and how he was beheaded. The interpreter translated everything wonderfully well until this point. Then he paused and, amidst an uproar of laughter from the audience, the interpreter said, in his own language of course, John the Baptist had his head amputated!!

The tour of Europe was the beginning of the wider outreach of Billy's ministry. From then on invitations started to pour into the Minneapolis headquarters asking Billy to conduct Crusades in every corner of the world. Exciting and humbling events tumbled over one another in Billy's life as he obeyed the command of God to go into all the world and preach the gospel. Billy's interest, however, didn't stop at preaching. Already the radio programme he had started was being broadcast all over the world, and his film company had made several films which were being used to bring men and women to a personal faith in Jesus Christ.

Starting from a small beginning, the films which are now produced by one of the subsidiary companies of the Billy Graham Evangelistic Association are translated into various languages, involving lip synchronization.

Lip synchronization is a fascinating process and means that someone has to study the lip movements of all the characters in the film and then take what they say in any particular language and translate it so that in the new language the movement of the mouth will correspond as near as possible to the movement of the mouth the actors made when the film was first shot. This technique is now being used to put the films which Billy sponsors into French, German and Spanish. By this means they have a much wider use and can be shown in many other parts of the world than those countries where English is spoken. Sometimes the films tell the life story of someone who came to know Jesus Christ through the Crusade. At other times documentary films are made, which portray the travels of Billy through many different countries.

And so Billy accepted some of the invitations to go to far-off countries to preach the Gospel.

In 1956 hundreds of people gathered at the Airport to sing hymns as Billy Graham reached Bombay Airport in India. These people had cheerful faces as they welcomed the evangelist to their city, but the city to which they welcomed him was not a very cheerful place. The newspapers described the happenings as the blackest days in the history of Bombay. The people were rioting as armed mobs stalked around the streets, killing people, overturning buses and cars, and stoning police officers to death. Billy was met by this sight as he started on his tour of India. Surely this was a city where the people needed to know the power of the Lord Jesus to transform their lives from hatred to love. Throughout the length and breadth of India he travelled, preaching in large towns, small villages, and to gatherings of missionaries.

As he was getting ready to leave the hotel in Bombay at the start of his visit, Billy was touched very deeply by an incident which happened. The time was just 6 a.m. and Billy and his team were hurrying away to catch a plane. Four ladies came in through the door of the hotel.

"We are missionaries," they said, "and have travelled several hundred miles to see you. We have ridden on old broken down trains for two days to hear you at one of your meetings, but the train had engine trouble and we didn't arrive in time. Please will you give us a brief message to take back to our people."

One of the missionaries told Billy that a Sunday School class of old women had been praying for months for the meetings in India.

"They sold their extra rice and sent ten rupees (about 14/-) to help towards the cost of the expenses of the meetings," she said.

Billy was overcome by this statement, for he had just seen a tremendous poverty among the people of India. Children were running about with swollen stomachs because they didn't have enough to eat. They had skinny legs and arms, and bodies covered in sores. Anyone who could sacrifice money meant for food in such a country must indeed be very devout. Billy swallowed hard and pulled out his Bible. He began to read to these missionaries, and there and then, in that hotel foyer, he held a short service. As Billy bowed his head in prayer the porters and the other guests who had gathered around to listen bowed their heads too. He prayed that God would make him worthy to minister to such devoted people. Rising from their seats the missionaries went back several hundred miles to their people, and Billy went on his way to the next meeting, and the hotel went back to its daily business.

Madras is a city in the south of India and people came from all parts of the country to attend the meetings there. One man walked over 400 miles, preaching along the way, in order to be present at the Crusade. At another place, the people themselves had gathered together to work and make a suitable place to hold the meetings. They had moved the earth entirely by hand, taking out the soil in baskets, until an arena arranged in tiers had been built.

Billy was greatly burdened, especially for the children of India, after seeing so much disease.

"My heart ached," he said to one of his friends, "as I realized a little bowl of rice to these children means everything. They don't have any doctors to come and help them when they get sick. They are not even able to buy medicine. I wish there was something we could do. There seems to be so little."

Then he remembered the words of Jesus when He said that if we offend even one of these little ones it would be better that a millstone had been wrapped around our necks and we were cast into the depths of the sea. What could be done for this great country? Only by making men and women and boys and girls realize their need of asking Jesus Christ into their lives can people begin to see that it is up to them, and up to each one of us, to help the poor and needy of this world. So, with 35,000 miles behind him, Billy turned for home. India, that land of mystery, had once again heard the gospel of Jesus Christ. And so, by way of the Philippines, Korea, Formosa and Japan, Billy reached his home once again.

* * *

The Statue of Liberty stands guard at the entrance to New York Harbour. The figure seems to stand defiantly over New York City, with its skyscrapers, large motor cars, and a hustle and bustle peculiarly all its own. Then there is Madison Square Gardens, a famous arena where great sporting events have taken place. This was the setting for what many people described as "almost a miracle", which took place in the summer of 1957. A circus had just finished using the Gardens prior to the meetings of Billy Graham and his team, and the familiar animal smell of circuses still hung in the air as the first meeting began. Week after week New Yorkers packed Madison Square Gardens to hear the message of salvation preached.

On the night of June 1st a telecast was made to the whole of the United States. There was an estimated audience of six to seven million listeners. This was more than could have been reached by preaching a whole year in Madison Square Garden itself. Some wonderful stories have been told of the New York Crusade.

One night a taxi driver was driving one of the Crusade staff to the meeting and he began running down Billy Graham. He used all the old arguments and went on and on at some length. The passenger could stand it no longer and gave a long lecture to the driver. That night as the Crusade worker was standing watching the crowds respond to the invitation he saw a face that he thought was vaguely familiar.

"Don't I know you?" he asked.

"Could be," the man replied.

"Perhaps we have done business together?"

"We sure have," said the man, "I drove the taxi tonight that brought you to the meeting."

All over the world people had been praying for this Crusade. In Hong Kong a little Chinese lady walked into one of the prayer meetings. After hearing of the needs of New York she gave her bracelet to help the finances of the Crusade. And because of these prayers, as it had happened all over the world, so it happened again in New York. God worked through His servant and many thousands of people came to know and love the Lord Jesus Christ.

It is not always easy to be an evangelist and someone once said that an evangelist must be many things to many people. The preacher for this work must have the heart of a lion, the patience of a donkey, the wisdom of an elephant, the industry of an ant, and as many lives as a cat.

Billy is separated from his family often for months on end. His wife stays at home, looking after the house and the children, but sometimes she manages to get away for a little while and join her husband at one of the meetings.

Only a very special sort of person would be able to manage in these circumstances. And Ruth Graham is a very special sort of person. Born in China of missionary parents she went to America to attend college and it was there she met Billy. She believes that God has called her to be the wife of an evangelist and, of course, her part is just as important in its way as Billy's more glamorous life.

6

IN THE STEPS OF DAVID LIVINGSTONE

THE Southern Cross Crusade. This was the title given to the meetings conducted in the lands "down under" when Billy and the team went to Australia and New Zealand in 1959 to conduct meetings there.

Just 171 years previously, the first settlers in Australia arrived in Port Jackson, which is now called Sydney. Three-quarters of the settlers were convicts, but they had brought with them their own chaplain. In 1793 the first church was built. It was a very primitive affair and when it was opened the whole structure had only cost the grand sum of £67 13s. 2½d. Where the odd half-penny came from nobody seems to know. Since then, of course, Australia has flourished and grown at a fantastic rate. It was to this vital new country that Billy came to preach to them the same old, yet ever new gospel.

For fifteen weeks Billy travelled up and down, from North to South, from East to West Australia, and New Zealand. This was not an easy Crusade, because Billy arrived in Australia under the supervision of his doctors. On their orders he had had to curtail some of the meetings at which he was scheduled to speak, as he was suffering from a very rare disease which affected the vision of his left eye. This had been caused by tiredness and over-work and it was a very tired Billy indeed who landed on Australian soil for the first time.

Through all these weeks the message of the Gospel went to every part of this great continent, and many can look back to this time as the moment when, for the first time, they put their faith and trust in Jesus Christ. Radio and television carried the message into the parts of the country where the team could not travel. In many parts of Australia there are vast areas where few people live. There are just very lonely "homesteads", where sheep farmers have no other neighbours for thousands of miles in each direction. The radio becomes to these people a very vital means, not only of entertainment, but of contact with the outside world. It is only by radio that the people in these isolated places can call for help when it is needed. And the Flying Doctor Service would not be able to function were it not for the use of radio. When people fall ill, they switch on their radio and speak to the nearest contact centre, where they know that help will be forthcoming as quickly as possible. And by radio, in these remote areas, the message of the Crusade meetings was transmitted to those who could not travel the great distances to attend the meetings.

The whole vision of a Crusade in the Southern Hemisphere was really the dream of one man—Archbishop Mowll, who died before the Crusade actually came into being. But Billy paid a great tribute to this man at the closing rally in Sydney, when with one of his characteristic gestures he pointed to the heavens and said:

"I believe you can see this great gathering here this afternoon, sir, and that it makes your heart glad to see your hopes fulfilled for the city which you loved and served so faithfully."

People from all walks of life were touched by this great crusade and at one of the meetings in Sydney a burglar, who had just completed a long prison sentence, came to hear Billy preach. Whilst in prison he had heard Billy's voice by Radio Relay. He had arranged to meet with a few of his friends one night and they had planned another robbery. On his way to meet them he decided he would call in at the meeting first to hear Billy in person and then go on to join his friends later. As Billy was preaching that night he said in the course of his sermon:

"You are not here by accident. You are here by divine appointment."

That night the burglar went forward to accept Christ as his Saviour. He still kept his appointment with his friends, but he went to tell them what had happened to him and not to join in their schemes for another burglary.

And so the stories came in from all over the country of men and women, and boys and girls, from all walks of life, coming face to face with the Saviour.

The time soon came for Billy and the team to leave Australia. Just before he left Billy was heard to remark to a friend:

"In generations to come they will look back on these days and say 'That was a revival'."

* * *

The following year Billy was off on his travels again, but this time to a very different continent. This was to be in many ways one of the most colourful and exciting trips that he had ever made. Africa was the destination of the team. Billy has described this continent as an awakening giant. In Africa, there are about seven hundred different languages and so there are great problems in communication. Many missionaries are working in this vast continent and they have laboured for many years telling the Africans of the love of the Lord Jesus Christ, so Billy was not going with a new message but, as he said, "I am coming to reap where others have sown." The plane took off from Idlewild Airport, New York, carrying Billy and the team, and the first stop on their tour was Monrovia, the capital of Liberia.

After a short stop at Dakar, the plane was on its way to Liberia, and as the plane made its descent towards the airport dense smoke poured from one of the engines.

"The plane's on fire," shouted one of the people gathered in the reception area at the airport.

"It looks as though it's coming in to try and make a landing," said his friend, turning to him.

"Yes, the aeroplane is beginning to lose height. It's coming in to the end of the runway. It seems to be coming down all right. The wheels have touched the runway."

Clang, Clang, Clang, sounded the bell, as the fire engine chased across the airport to be on hand.

A great sigh of relief came from all those safely on the ground as the plane eventually came to a stop and the passengers were able to climb out, unhurt. The cause of the smoke was soon found to be oil spurting against the hot metal, but this was to set a pattern for the eventful tour through this vast continent.

One of the most interesting sights that Billy saw in Liberia was a display of tribal dancing. One of the dancers was covered completely in a grass costume from head to foot and was supposed to represent the "country devil". He kept dancing up to the party of men and tapping Billy on the chin, saying, "I am the devil, give me a dollar."

Billy's reply was quick and to the point. "I have come to cast out the devil," he retorted.

The next stop on the tour was Ghana. In colourful costumes and in all kinds of transport men and women came from all over the country to attend the meetings. In Nigeria the chief of one of the tribes told how he had come to know Jesus Christ when he was a boy of ten years old. Then the talking drums, which can speak in the tonal language of the tribe, welcomed Billy to their village.

The chief told Billy, "Some day, I hope to lay my crown at Jesus's feet."

One of the smallest, yet one of the most inspiring meetings of the whole tour took place in a little village in Nigeria. They call it the "Village on the

Rocks" and Billy was told the story of the village on his way to visit the people there. Many of the villagers are Christians and the ruler of the area, a Muslim, was very disturbed when he heard that the villagers had built themselves a tiny mud church. He told them that they must close the church, but the villagers replied that they must worship their Lord and would continue to do so, until he threw them in jail. One day a group of young men came to the village armed with knives and threatened the villagers, but the Christian leader of the village stood firm face to face with the toughs, and spoke to them quietly.

"Over there are our crops," he said. "You may burn them if you wish. Over there are our homes and you can tear them down if you must." Then he opened his loose robe at the neck and said, "Here are our lives, you can kill us, but you cannot take our Christ from us."

This was more than the young hooligans could stand and letting their weapons fall to their sides they crept away. This, then, was the village where Billy was bound to join in their worship. The little church would only hold about forty people and the little clearing round about was full with another hundred people. Some of the congregation had walked fifteen miles just to be there on that Sunday morning. Billy was greatly touched and deeply moved as he left the service that day.

* * *

"Just look down there," said Billy, with great glee. "A great herd of elephants."

Sure enough, beneath the plane, elephants galloped off to escape the great monster from above as the plane zoomed low above their heads. Buffalo, zebra, and antelope were also plainly to be seen. The plane was on its way to the town of Livingstone, named after the famous missionary, David Livingstone, who first discovered the Victoria Falls. Amongst the many who heard Billy speak in that little town were some students from a teacher training college, which had also been named after the famous missionary.

David Livingstone was never far from Billy's mind as he toured this part of Africa. As he stood above the great Victoria Falls and gazed on their beauty he could easily understand why the Scottish missionary had called this sight the most wonderful of all his travels.

Standing at the foot of Livingstone's statue on the edge of the Falls, he thought back on the loneliness and great hardships the missionaries had endured as they sought to open up the great continent for

Christianity and in some measure to bring civilization to the "dark continent".

"I am not worthy to polish the shoes of missionary heroes like Livingstone and Mary Slessor," Billy said. "I am deeply moved and grateful for the privilege of reaping where they sowed."

One day as Billy was walking along the bank of the Zambesi River, he came across a film crew making a film called *Livingstone's Last Journey*. The director offered Billy a ride in a stretcher-like contraption similar to the one in which the explorer had made his last, final trek into the interior of the continent. David Livingstone had been at the end of his life and in a very weak condition when he was carried along in this way by two bearers, each carrying the end of the two long poles on which the stretcher rested. Billy accepted the ride wanting to know what it felt like to be swung from side to side as the bearers walked along. His sympathies went out to David Livingstone who had had to endure this form of transport. The little jaunt very nearly ended in disaster. As they were going along the banks of the river, one of the poles broke and Billy just managed to stop himself from falling into the water and giving an unexpected lunch to the crocodiles.

Before setting off on the tour of Africa, Billy

had thought a great deal of David Livingstone and what he had achieved in his lifetime. After seeing something of the great results of his own Crusades and people coming to know the Lord Jesus, Billy said, "If that great heart of African exploration is watching our Crusade in Africa from the battlements of Heaven, I trust he will know that we have not forgotten. We follow in his train and in the train of the Master whose he was and whom he served."

After speaking at the meetings in Nairobi Billy boarded yet another plane, and after they had been in the air for a few minutes Billy looked out of the window of the plane and saw a wonderful sight. Below him was a school for missionaries' children and the children were jumping about all over the field, waving and shouting. In their midst they had arranged rocks to spell out a message for Billy and all his team. The huge letters read "God bless you all". The party was strangely silent as the plane droned on through the sky.

A great giant of a chief, six feet seven inches tall, sat on the platform at the meeting in Usumburu as Billy preached to a crowd of the subjects of the chief, all huge warriors like himself. The team's arrival in this part of Africa was the most hazardous of the tour. The pilot of the plane was flying the route for the very first time. High mountains were all around the country and thick clouds blacked out the view in all directions. There was still another 150 miles to go to their destination and both radios on the plane went dead. There were some very tense moments as the team held a prayer meeting. The members of the press on board joined the loudest in the "Hallelujah" as a hole came in the clouds right above their destination.

As the giant chief, a member of the Watutsi tribe, was leaving the meeting, some of his subjects pressed around him very closely, clapping and cheering. Billy, who knows what it feels like to be trapped in a huge crowd, was very anxious for the safety of the chief. Wading into the crowd he tried to clear a path through the great throng of people, but just then the chief reached the safety of his car.

* * *

Bethlehem, Jerusalem and the other places Jesus visited whilst He was here on earth, had only been names to Billy until now. But on his way back from Africa he paid a visit to the Holy Land. This was a tremendous experience for him as he walked in the spots where Jesus had walked and saw some of the places mentioned in the Bible.

And so he turned his face to home. After travelling for so long through the changing continent of Africa he looked back on the thousands of miles and the many thousands of people who had come to his meetings and he thought of the problems facing the world today.

"Only as men receive the love of God shed abroad on Calvary can they work together to solve the problems that plague the entire world."

This was his prayer. In future days he was to see more of the problems as he sought by the preaching of the Gospel to change men and women so that these problems would cease to exist.

7

BACK TO EUROPE

How would it feel to go to church in someone else's house and when you got there you would only see the neighbours from your own street? What would you think if there were no Sunday School for you to attend on a Sunday? Suppose you could not buy a church magazine or a Christian newspaper?

These are some of the things you would have to endure if you lived in East Germany. And this was the way things were in September 1960 when Billy was invited to conduct a series of meetings in Berlin.

At that time no wall had been built to divide East Berlin from West Berlin and during the Crusade it was possible for people who lived in East Berlin to cross the boundary and worship in the tent which had been specially erected in the Western half of the city. The people streamed in from the East, often defying the police, for even at that time it was difficult, though not impossible, to cross from one side of the city to the other. Some nights as many as 2,000 East Berliners found their way into the meetings. There were delays, sometimes of hours, at the various checkpoints. Those coming from the East could not spend East German money in the Western part of Berlin and so they were provided with food by the Crusade officials.

"You have twenty-four hours to get out of town," was the message given to Billy Graham by the East Berlin police. But the Crusade went on in what was described as the "world's largest tent". It was specially designed and built for the Crusade. 18,000 square yards of cloth were needed for the tent, which held 20,000 people, and 22 miles of rope were used to hold the tent in position!

As the East Berliners tried to return home they were held up for hours and sometimes stripped of their passports. This caused a great deal of hardship, for without their passports the people could not obtain food.

Many people wrote letters of appreciation to Mr. Graham, but this one surely speaks for them all.

"Dear Mr. Graham," it reads, "I am a German girl, nearly fourteen years old, and I listened to you on five evenings. I want to thank you very much, because your sermons showed me the way to Jesus. Many people and I hope to hear and see you in

Hamburg next year again. Many birthday greetings, Yours truly."

It is not easy to be a Christian in East Berlin and those who returned to their homes after surrendering their lives to Jesus Christ would soon learn something of what it must have felt like to be a Christian in the first century.

And so the story continues. All over the United States, South America, the Far East and back again to Britain. In 1961 Billy Graham came back to Britain. This time he made his way to the north of England where the industrial heart of the country lies. Manchester was his destination and there he had a most unfortunate setback. For the first week of the three week period of the Crusade, the meetings went on without him. Billy was lying ill in a hotel room in London suffering from a severe throat infection, which had plagued him before and which was to go on recurring for some time. Of course, with an infected throat he could not preach, and his place was taken at the meetings in Manchester by his brother-in-law, Leighton Ford.

Manchester has always been thought of as a cold, damp place, and the month of May 1961 was no exception. Manchester stands at the heart of England's industrial area and its main business for the past seven centuries has been to produce manufactured cotton products. Linked by ship canal to the great port of Liverpool, the city of Manchester is much more than a textile centre. Since the Industrial Revolution it has sent its exports of iron and steel, machinery and locomotives, paper, glass and rubber products to every part of the world, and its treeless crowded streets were the setting for the Crusade in May 1961. But, as Billy found out, the environment does not touch too greatly the million people who inhabit the city.

Since the days when Manchester was a Roman fort, it has exercised a great influence over the surrounding north of England. In the days when the Roman Legionnaires inhabited the countryside, the soldiers of Julius Caesar were writing home and complaining about the endless rain. In spite of the rain, many people in Manchester responded to the invitation to know for themselves the love and the saving power of the Lord Jesus Christ. Again, as had been done in London, telephone relays were set up to every part of the country, linking the Maine Road Football Ground with churches and centres around the British Isles. From as far away as Guernsey to the Hebridean Islands, people were listening in to the telephone relays.

But what do these Crusade meetings really

achieve? Let us look at the Manchester Crusade in detail to learn more of the Billy Graham story. 416,500 people attended the three weeks of meetings in Maine Road Football Stadium. Of that number 17,867 responded to the invitation to accept Jesus Christ as their Saviour. The members of Billy's team took forty factory meetings in and around the city of Manchester. There were 1,400 telephone relays to the various centres around the country. At the closing service 50,000 people were present to listen to the message and, on one day when the service was televised, there were ten million people looking in.

It has been said that Billy Graham has preached to more people than any other living person. This is most probably correct, but at the same time it carries a great responsibility, for he has to be very sure himself that he is right in the centre of God's will, that he is preaching to the audience not what he wants to tell them, but what God would have him tell the people. Every moment and every part of his life is given over to wanting to win men and women and boys and girls to a saving knowledge of the Lord Jesus Christ. This is why Billy Graham is preaching today. The statistics showed that on the special youth nights, when sometimes 2,300 people per evening would come forward to find out more about the Christian life, nearly 80% of those who responded were committing their lives to Jesus Christ for the first time.

But what happens to these people? First of all, they are spoken to by a trained counsellor who wants to help them and to make sure they understand the seriousness of the step they have just taken. Then they are given special literature to help them to grow in the Christian life which they have just started. The counsellor who spoke to them in the first place promises to keep in touch with them to answer their queries and to make sure that they are settling down into the life of a church. This is the most important part, for all these people are put into touch straight away with the church for which they state a preference. The minister of the church is asked to contact that person immediately and to encourage them to attend church.

Many of these people who come forward at the meetings have never seen a Bible before, and the very first thing they do is to rush out and buy one so that they can start to read God's Word for themselves.

It is not all large crowds, and sometimes there are moments of despondency. When some of Mr. Graham's associates were speaking at special meetings in the great engineering plants of the

Manchester area they found themselves preaching in very unusual places. Sometimes they were completely ignored, and sometimes, whilst they were preaching, the men would gradually walk away until they found themselves talking to fresh air.

What happens before a Crusade begins? For many months before Mr. Graham arrives in a city, a great deal of work has gone on behind the scenes to make sure that everything is ready for his arrival. A special office will have been set up to deal with all the correspondence which arises as soon as it is announced that a Crusade is to take place. Then, and this is by far the most important thing, prayer partners are enrolled. These are people from the immediate area of the Crusade and sometimes from far afield as well, who promise to pray regularly for all the preparations of the Crusade. They promise to pray, too, for the unseen thousands who will go to the Crusade meetings night by night. They promise to pray for Billy Graham, that God will uphold him and give him the right words to speak.

In Manchester, Billy's wife, Ruth, gave a very amusing side-light on the prayer partners for the Crusade. As Billy was not able to be in Manchester for the first week, all the prayer partners had been asked to pray for his speedy recovery and when, on the night when Ruth Graham stood beside her husband on the platform, she was asked to say a few words to the thousands of people in the stadium, she referred to Billy's recent illness and said:

"It just shows the position men hold in this world. Can you imagine hundreds of people praying that a woman would get her voice back again?"

Money has to be raised as well, because it costs a great deal to run the Crusades. Rent for the stadium has to be found and sometimes this rent can cost many thousands of pounds. All the literature which has to be sent out has to be paid for, as well as the literature which is given to the inquirers; and so it goes on. But Billy himself never takes a penny from these Crusades, because he receives a salary from his Association. So all the money that is given for a Crusade goes for the purpose for which it was intended. This is the formula for the Crusades, whether they take place in Britain, the United States, in Europe, or in any other place where an invitation goes out to Billy.

At the Crusade in Manchester many of the young people who surrendered their lives to Jesus Christ had been brought by friends.

One of the outstanding preparations for any Crusade is the "Operation Andrew" programme. In the Bible we read of the way in which Jesus called his disciples. First of all, Andrew heard the

Master speak and rushed to find his brother, Simon Peter. The Bible says, "And he brought him to Jesus."

This is the way "Operation Andrew" works. Someone has a friend who does not know Jesus and they begin to pray for this friend. Then they are invited along to one of the meetings.

Joyce was travelling to her work one day when she met a friend of hers, Sylvia. She hadn't seen Sylvia for some time and had been warned that the friend had gone "all religious". They chatted together and then Sylvia asked Joyce if she was doing anything on the Saturday night. Joyce was immediately on her guard.

"She's trying to get me along to a religious meeting," she thought. Out loud Joyce said, "I'm not doing anything in particular."

"Would you like to go to hear Billy Graham in Manchester then?"

Seeing the look on Joyce's face, Sylvia went on, "It's all right, it's quite free—there's a coach from church going."

On the journey Joyce couldn't help noticing how happy all the people around her seemed to be. Eventually they arrived at Manchester and, as usual, it was raining.

All through the message Joyce sat with a battle

raging inside her. At the end, when Billy gave the invitation Joyce turned to Sylvia and said quietly,

"I'm going up Sylvia."

So Joyce joined the many hundreds walking their way to the front.

On the coach home Sylvia was able to help Joyce more and told her again that Christ had died for her sins on the cross. Joyce knew she was a sinner and asked the Lord to cleanse her. It was not the same Joyce who returned to her home that night, but a different person.

"Since then," she says, "Christ has kept me and lovingly cared for me. I teach in Sunday School and spend my holidays on a Beach Mission. The Lord becomes more precious every day."

8

TEAM WORK

During the years, Billy has gathered round him an amazing team of men. They are drawn from many backgrounds, races and cultures, but they all have one thing in common with Billy, and that is the desire to see men and women coming to know Christ as their Saviour.

Billy himself is the first to admit that he would not be able to lead such vast Crusades were it not for the untiring help of those around him. Each Crusade meeting is the work of a team and Billy is just a part of it.

The platform team are the ones mostly in the public eye. On these four men depends the entire programme until Billy steps to the microphone to begin his sermon. Cliff Barrows leads the singing and generally conducts the proceedings. Then George Beverly Shea sings in his familiar baritone voice. He believes that a message can be given in song as clearly as a sermon, and his songs are carefully chosen to lead into the message Billy will bring later in the programme.

Two musicians make up this part of the team,

and Don Hustad on the organ, and Tedd Smith at the piano, both know what is required of them.

Other men are at work in various parts of the world, organizing Crusade meetings and preaching to the crowds who attend. Many years ago, Billy realized that it is far better to have someone of your own race to preach to you. Often the message is more readily accepted if the crowds know that the preacher is one of their own countrymen.

On Billy Graham's staff is an evangelist from Africa who spends a good deal of his time working on radio programmes in Liberia. Then there is an Indian, another African, and a Spanish-speaking evangelist from South America. There are men, too, who go to a town or city to conduct a small Crusade. They preach for five or six nights and then Billy joins them for a large, final meeting. These men are doing valuable work and, because they can take these meetings, Billy is able to travel round more and visit places he would not otherwise be able to visit.

All the men are great friends and when they can all meet together (which is not often) a good deal of friendly teasing goes on. One of Billy's colleagues, T. W. Wilson, will not be allowed to forget the following incident in a hurry. (Everyone calls

Mr. Wilson by his initials and so he is just T.W. to his friends.)

Billy had just returned from Hawaii where he had not been very well. He and T.W. were driving to their homes in North Carolina and it was a cold, wet, miserable night.

As Billy was still feeling a bit groggy he decided to lie down on the back seat of the car and try to get some sleep. They had been driving for sometime in pitch darkness along an expressway when T. W. Wilson pulled the car into a garage for some petrol. Glancing over his shoulder, he saw that Billy was still asleep and not wanting to disturb him he got out of the car and decided to have a cup of coffee.

A few moments later, Billy woke up and realizing that T.W. had gone inside the café decided to get out of the car to stretch his legs. No sooner had he gone than T.W. came out of the café and, without looking in the back of the car, jumped into the driving seat, started the engine, took off the brake and raced off on the road to home. Billy returned to where he had left the car just in time to see the red tail-lights disappearing down the road.

There he was on a rainy night without any overcoat, stranded in a strange café miles away from any form of civilization. Just then a truck driver came out and Billy persuaded him to try and catch up with the car now completely out of sight. With Billy beside him, the truck driver urged his vehicle forward but it was just not fast enough to catch up with the more powerful car.

They turned round and went back to the café. Inside, Billy tried to hire a car, only to discover that there was no car available in the area.

"Anyway, what's your name?" said the man behind the café counter.

"Billy Graham."

"Oh, yeah, I've heard that one before," said the bartender in a disbelieving voice.

It took Billy some considerable time to get the man to believe that he really *was* Billy Graham. Eventually, he was persuaded and after a great deal of explanations a man was finally found who agreed to drive Billy to an airport near his home, where he would be able to hire a car to drive himself the last few miles home.

It was a very tired Billy who eventually steered the car through the gates of his house. And what a sight met him! T. W. Wilson and Billy's wife were both outside in a very agitated state. It was only as he was nearing the end of the journey that T.W. thought to take a look at the back seat. On finding it empty he couldn't think what to do and in his agitation he called out the State Police, the F.B.I., the Highway Patrol and sundry other officers of the law.

The incident ended peacefully, but the rest of the team won't let T. W. Wilson forget it very quickly.

On another occasion, just after the Manchester Crusade, one team member nearly lost all his luggage. Billy had been invited to speak at St. Martins-in-the-Bull-Ring in Birmingham one Sunday morning. He wanted to go straight on from there to London but didn't want to be hindered with all his suitcases. He asked one member of the team if he would drive back to London and take all his luggage and some belonging to other members of the team as well.

The car was piled high with suitcases, dictating machines, typewriters, and sundry small packets. There was barely room for the driver as the car sped south to await Billy's arrival at the hotel in London. The driver looked rather sheepish and shame-faced when he discovered that, in his anxiety and worry to make sure he had got everything from Manchester, he had forgotten to bring his own luggage. His clothes were still hanging behind the bedroom door in Manchester, and he only had the clothes he stood up in until the rest of his belongings were sent down by train from Manchester.

Some members of Billy's trusted helpers never have their names in print or appear before thousands of people. These are the men who spend long months away from their homes and families, preparing the ground for a series of Crusade meetings.

They are known as Crusade Directors. Theirs is a hard task, for they go into a city and have to start all the preparations from scratch. Very often they have to find a site for the meetings and this is no easy matter. Most large halls and open air stadia are often booked up for years ahead, but a great deal of prayer goes into every movement and the Lord marvellously opens doors. What has seemed an impossibility a short while ago becomes a reality as the way is opened up.

An office has to be found and staff engaged to deal with the countless details which form the preparations. Churches have to be contacted and prayer support enlisted. All too soon the months have slipped by and the great day is here at last. Billy Graham arrives in that particular city, knowing that all the details have been worked out and that he can apply himself wholeheartedly to preaching the Gospel.

Then as soon as the Crusade is over the Crusade Director is off again. Perhaps he will be on his way across the world to start all the preparations again.

Billy knows that his work could not be nearly so effective without this team behind him. They take a great deal of the responsibility off his shoulders so that he can spend his time in study and listening to God's voice directing him the next step. Every week he has to record a twenty-minute sermon for his radio programme and this goes on, week in and week out. Even when he is in the midst of a Crusade the recording has to be made. Then, perhaps, he records in his hotel bedroom or perhaps he is preaching in the sand in the middle of a desert. Wherever it is, Cliff Barrows will not be far away as he edits and perfects the finished tape.

It could be that Billy has to appear on television or take part in a film that is being made. Or maybe he is off to lecture at some college or university. Whatever he is doing, the prime force of his life is never far away and he will always seek an opportunity of presenting the claims of Jesus Christ to his hearers.

Everyone has to have some recreation, and one of Billy's favourite pastimes is golf. He has boundless energy, and his father's comment about him as a child is still true.

"Billy Frank," he said, "will never sit still long enough to be a farmer. He'll probably make a good salesman."

In a way, that is exactly what he is. But he is selling the world's richest commodity. Whenever a man or a woman or a boy or a girl turns and accepts the Lord Jesus as their Saviour then Billy experiences a little of what could be called satisfaction.

He will never be wholly satisfied, however, whilst there are still people in the world who do not know the power that comes from accepting Jesus Christ.

* * *

The name of Hollywood, California, conjures up for most people a scene of famous film stars, cowboy heroes, and Walt Disney characters. This is the part of the world where a great number of films are made.

Close by the Walt Disney Studios a modern new building stands. An illuminated sign on one of the walls says "World Wide Pictures". This is the studio where all the Billy Graham films are made. It is from here the films are written and directed. All over the world these films are used as part of Billy's ministry. Many hundreds of thousands of showings take place during a year in all parts of the world.

In Australia, New Zealand, France, Germany, England and wherever a projector can be bought or borrowed the Gospel message is told through these films. Some of the films which have been made as part of Billy's ministry tell the stories of the various Crusades, some tell the story of a person who came to know Jesus Christ at a Crusade meeting, and some are films where Billy preaches a short message. Whatever the theme might be, there are many people around the world who can tell the story of how they found Jesus at a film showing.

These films are also used in preparation for Crusades that are being planned. In an area around the city holding the Crusade, the films go to interested churches and groups so that they can see exactly what will take place when the Crusade finally begins.

Literature, too, plays an important part in Billy's life. He knows that all over the world men and women are longing to read something, and if that something can be a piece of Christian literature then there is an opportunity to win that person for the Lord Jesus.

In 1960, Billy launched the magazine *Decision*, which he prayed would one day spread to all parts of the world and be translated into many languages, so that people everywhere could learn more of the Bible and what it has to say to each individual. He is beginning to see his prayer come true as *Decision* is now published in seven editions, in four languages, month by month.

Billy believes in using every means he can to preach the Gospel, and by using radio, television, films and the printed page, the message is being spread.

If one day someone were to invent a new means of communication Billy Graham would be amongst the first to use it for God's glory.

9

LOOKING TO THE FUTURE

IN 1962 Billy and the team went south. South America, that great continent of contrasts, where from the four corners they came to hear the message of the gospel. Dark-faced Indian men wearing sandals trudged scores of miles over rocky highways for the privilege of hearing this preacher. Indian women, walking barefoot, carrying their babies on their backs, plodded slightly behind their men folk, for this is the custom in South America. Of course, here again, Billy's message had to be translated into Spanish for the benefit of those who were there. But the message was still the same, the never changing message of the gospel. From place to place, city to city, the message of the cross is proclaimed.

So, once again, Billy headed for Europe and this time his destination was the country across the English Channel.

The land of France, so near to England, and yet in so many ways very different. The country has had a very interesting and turbulent history. During the 16th century, Protestant preachers came to the country from Switzerland and converted about one-eighth of the population. But persecution soon followed and this small minority, known as the Huguenots, were killed or imprisoned. Those who escaped these fates fled abroad to more security. But today the Protestants in France enjoy peace and security.

It was as the guns were echoing in the fields of France in 1918 that Billy Graham was born, and it was to this land now bathed in peace and freedom that he came in 1963 to preach the wonderful message of salvation. He had paid a brief visit to Paris in 1955, but this Crusade was vastly different. The land of France had changed in the years between and now a measure of prosperity had come to the country after the ravages of the Second World War.

Though the Protestants are still in the minority in France, yet they were on tiptoe and eager to win others to the Lord Jesus Christ.

So on that Sunday in May all was in readiness at the Porte de Clignancourt. Situated on the outskirts of Paris, the huge tent used in Germany before had been brought across the country and pitched on the open space of what is commonly known as "The Flea Market". As the market finished its business each evening the people stayed on and waited until it was time for the service to begin. And the people came and committed their lives to Christ. Not just Frenchmen, but people from all over the world were there. From Madagascar, from Germany, from England, and New Zealand, they came to hear the message that is universal.

From a camp nearby a group of gipsies in their gay, colourful clothes came to hear, the tramps of Paris in their filthy rags, who sleep in the streets of Paris each evening wrapped in newspapers, came to hear.

From the Protestants of Paris the choir was recruited and, under the leadership of Cliff Barrows, all those who were there thrilled to hear the French voices raised in singing, "A toi la gloire, O Ressuscité" (To thee the glory, O Risen One).

As the rats from the market place ran across the floor of the tent, the people of Paris heard and received the Gospel message.

The team turned their faces to other towns and cities in France and from each one came news that, as in Paris, so in the other places, the French people sought to help their fellow countrymen to find eternal life.

* * *

In recent years Billy has been very troubled and distressed at the race riots in his own country. He has made a special point of taking meetings in the troubled South. In 1965, he cancelled a private visit to England in order to preach in the cities of strife in the Southern States of America.

Montgomery, Alabama, was the setting for an eight-day Crusade in June 1965. An invitation had been sent to him by the combined clergy of the city. No one knew quite what to expect as there had been a great many disturbances in that area.

All was quiet during the meetings and Billy was heard to remark: "The only need we had of policemen was to direct traffic."

A clergyman said: "Montgomery is going to be a better place to live. Something has happened to our hearts through the preaching of this Crusade."

The Gospel speaks the same message to every person in the world. Whether he be black, brown, yellow or white, he still needs to know that Jesus Christ died for him. And Billy has proved that where people accept this message they can begin to live in harmony with one another. Wherever he goes his advice is sought by leaders of nations who can see no hope for this troubled world. Billy tells them that there is only one hope and that hope is Jesus Christ.

And so Billy Graham preaches on. His Crusades are not so long now as they were a few years ago. The infections and illnesses he has suffered over the years have forced his doctors to tell him to ease up a little. Whereas just five or six years ago he would hold meetings for three months at a time and speak to innumerable gatherings during the day as well, now no Crusade lasts for more than a month, and he has cut his other engagements down to a minimum.

But he is not ready to give up. For as long as the Lord needs him he is ready to go on.

Early in 1964 a group of London business men met for lunch one day. As they sat around the table they began to talk about the wonderful ways in which God worked during the days of Harringay Crusade, just ten years previously. As they talked, their thoughts turned to the present day and they resolved to ask Billy Graham to return to London yet again to conduct a Crusade in 1966. An invitation was drawn up and signed by all those present.

The parchment scroll was then given to Billy in America and he replied that he would be pleased to accept the invitation.

A great question then arose. "Where could the Crusade take place?" Harringay Arena which was used in 1954 was no longer available. It was now just a warehouse. All the major sites in London were visited and talked over. It had to be a large place because Billy was only coming for one month, instead of three months as in 1954.

At last everyone was agreed that Earls Court Arena was the right place. The Arena holds 20,000 people and it is possible for a further 7,000 to watch the proceedings on closed-circuit television. From all parts of Britain letters of invitation poured in, asking Billy to take meetings in the North, South, East and West. Obviously he could not take all the meetings, so again the question came up, "What could be done?"

After a great deal of discussion it was decided that closed-circuit television should be used around the country as well as in Earls Court. The television pictures would measure 24 ft. by 18 ft. and would be shown in cinemas or large halls in various centres.

The committee responsible for the preparation was soon busy at work and thousands of prayer partners were enrolled. The offices were buzzing with volunteer helpers who were doing all the jobs involved with sending out letters to those who had promised to pray. After they had finished their own day's work they cheerfully worked through the evening at the Crusade Offices.

They come from all walks of life. Typists, secretaries, bus drivers, nurses, and bank clerks, work happily side by side. There is a blind man who can put letters into envelopes at a speed which makes those who can see look lazy. He is helping because he knows that the work he is doing is God's work. A Chelsea Pensioner in his bright red coat and medal ribbons adds a touch of colour to the office. Incidentally, this man is a never-tiring witness in the Chelsea Hospital where he lives and has shown several Billy Graham films to his fellow pensioners.

Billy is deeply convinced that it is only by the prayers of the countless thousands around the world that he can carry on preaching in the way he does. Speaking of the Harringay Crusade he said:

"There is only one explanation to that phenomenal campaign—prayer. We could even tell when people were letting down ever so slightly in their praying. We became extremely sensitive to the prayers of God's people everywhere.

"As we return to Great Britain, the responsibilities and opportunities are even greater than before. We return this time with far more fear and trembling. Therefore, in the Name of Christ, we are calling upon Christians everywhere to pray as you have never prayed before."

But the story does not end here. In a sense,

the story has only just begun. As long as there are men and women who need to know what Jesus Christ can do for them, then Billy Graham will be there, for he is obeying his Heavenly Father.

Very nearly the last words that Jesus spoke on this earth were "Go ye into all the world and preach the Gospel to every creature." Billy Graham has surely fulfilled this command.